Redeemed
From Shame

Redeemed
From Shame

Denise Renner

TEACH ALL NATIONS

A book company anointed
to take God's Word
to you and to the nations
of the world.

A division of
*RICK RENNER
MINISTRIES*

Unless otherwise indicated, all Scripture
quotations are taken from the *King James
Version* of the Bible.

Redeemed From Shame
ISBN 10-digit: 0-9725454-5-X
ISBN 13-digit: 978-0-9725454-5-7
Copyright © 2004 by Denise Renner
P. O. Box 702040
Tulsa, OK 74170-2040

Editorial Consultant: Cynthia D. Hansen
Cover Design: design@ZoeLifeCreative.com

Table of Contents

1

Healed and Delivered!

Have you ever suffered from feelings of shame and humiliation? Have you ever felt rejected and alone? Most people have felt this way from time to time. Please allow me to share my testimony with you of how God delivered me of a long-term physical condition and the emotional scars that were attached to it.

For many long years, I was held captive in a prison of shame without even realizing it. I want to share with you how God delivered me from the invisible prison that I suffered in for so much of my life. I am sharing my story with you for two reasons: because I want to give glory to God, and because I believe it will help you realize that, through Jesus' powerful work on the Cross, you can also be delivered from shame.

I grew up in a Christian home in Miami, Oklahoma, and went to church every Sunday and Wednesday. But when I was about twelve years old, I developed a serious case of cystic acne on my face and neck. I'm not talking about a normal case of teenage acne with a blemish here or there. Cystic acne is a very painful condition that penetrates through all five layers of the skin. The sores were often so deep and big that, when pressed upon, they would bruise.

For the next thirteen years, I would suffer in many ways from this terrible skin condition. I was made fun of in school. My peers accepted me for my singing voice and my personality, but not my looks. As I grew older, I was even turned down for desirable jobs because of my face.

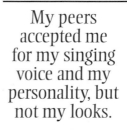

My peers accepted me for my singing voice and my personality, but not my looks.

Then in 1977 when I was twenty-four years old, I moved from Norman, Oklahoma (where I had studied at the University of Oklahoma and obtained a Music Education degree), to Houston, Texas. There I began to sing with the Houston Opera, working in the day and singing at night. It was in Houston as I drove to and from work that I first heard both Kenneth E. Hagin and Kenneth Copeland teach on First Peter 2:24: *"...by whose* [Jesus'] *stripes, ye were healed."*

> After being sick for so long, my mind had begun to adjust to the sickness.

Although I had been filled with the Holy Spirit since I was in college, I had never heard this teaching before — and it came just in time. After be-ing sick for so long, my mind had begun to adjust to the sickness. In fact, something in my personality had changed, causing me to believe that I wasn't as good as other people.

Instead of renewing my mind with what the Word of God said about my skin condition and my right to healing, I had begun to think that the condition was simply a part of life that I was meant to live with. The invisible curtain of shame had begun its work to bring its dom-inating presence over my soul.

> My journey to healing started with my own confession of faith.

After hearing this wonderful message, I decided to take hold of this wonderful truth about divine healing, and that truth began the process of setting me free. As Jesus said in John 8:32, *"And ye shall know the truth, and the truth shall make you free."*

My journey to healing started with my own confession of faith. Out of my mouth, out loud, morning, noon, and night, I'd confess that by the stripes of Jesus, I was healed. I'd look in the mirror at my face and boldly declare, "By His stripes, I am healed!" Over and over, I'd even sing, "By His stripes, I am healed." Those words of faith were on my lips all the time!

'Do You Really Want To Be Healed?'

After confessing the Word of God for about a month — every day, many times a day — I still couldn't see any change in my condition. Nevertheless, although I could not see God's hand at work, He was moving on my behalf. One day I was driving my car in Houston and listening to a radio preacher when suddenly it was as if the Holy Ghost spoke right through her to me. (Has this ever happened to you? Well, it happened to me!) She asked, *"Do you really want to be healed?"*

I knew beyond a shadow of a doubt that the Holy Ghost was asking me that question through this woman radio preacher. As I quietly sat there in my car, the Holy Spirit brought out His powerful searchlight and began exposing what was in my heart.

"Do you really want to be healed?"

You see, throughout all those years of trying to treat this skin condition, I went from doctor to doctor and tried antibiotic after antibiotic and treatment after treatment without seeing any change. After a while, I began to feel sorry for myself. As I sat there in my car, the Holy Spirit showed me that my own self-pity had been keeping me in bondage to this disease.

Can you imagine? I had been living with a "poor me" attitude for a very long time. At that moment, I repented. I asked God to forgive me and cleanse me of such selfishness, and I told Him that I definitely wanted to be healed.

> You cannot enjoy your self-pity and believe for your healing at the same time.

I didn't know it then, but I know it now: *You cannot enjoy your self-pity and believe for your healing at the same time.* You must give that "poor me" attitude to God and then repent of it, turn from it, and resist it with all your strength. Only then will you be able to receive power and anointing to stand strong in your faith and believe God for your healing.

14

Redeemed From Shame

Soon after that moment I experienced with the radio preacher and the Holy Spirit, I moved from Houston back to Oklahoma, still standing in faith for the manifestation of my healing. I was dating my future husband Rick at this time. It was wonderful to have such a loving boyfriend who accepted me just as I was. (I just wanted to add this note about Rick because it is true and because I love him so much after many years of marriage.)

My fight of faith against cystic acne was almost over. At this time, I was twenty-five years old and again living in Oklahoma. I went to bed one night, confessing once again that by Jesus' stripes, I was healed. It seemed like a normal night, but it was anything but that. *This was to be the night of my miracle.*

> I never suffered from that terrible skin condition again.

After thirteen years of pain, embarrassment, and one doctor after another, I was about to be free forever from this horrible condition. I had often felt like the woman with the issue of blood in Luke 8:43, who had spent *"...all her living upon physicians, neither could be healed of any."* But on this night I, like her, would receive a life-changing touch from Jesus.

I don't know if Jesus took two seconds, two minutes, four hours, or the entire night to perform my miracle. I just know that when I went to bed, I had cystic acne on my face and neck as had been the case for thirteen years — and when I awoke the next morning and looked in the mirror, my face and neck were completely clear. In fact, so much infection had left my face that my friends thought I had lost weight!

I slapped my blemish-free face in utter amazement and joy; then I called my mother on the phone and exclaimed, *"Mom, the Lord healed me! Jesus totally healed me and delivered me during the night!"*

From that moment on, I never suffered from that terrible skin condition again. I also cursed that sickness and commanded it to never come near my future children. Today I have three sons. And I can tell you with certainty that they will *never* suffer from that condition!

New Light on Hidden Shame

The day that God healed me, I didn't know about believing for scars to be removed. I didn't even think about it! As a result, the scars on my face from thirteen years of suffering from cystic acne remained — scars so deep that they went through all five layers of the skin.

As the years passed by and I reached my 40s, I also noticed that my face was beginning to fall years before most women deal with such problems. For years, I'd been forced to constantly pull on my face as I treated those terrible blemishes, and that had stolen from my youth.

Then in 2002, my husband Rick said to me, "Denise, let's just see what laser surgery can do to help eliminate the scars." We looked into the matter and discovered that lifting my face would also help make my scars less visible. Rick and I discussed the possibility of going further, and he said, "Honey, let's allow the surgeon to do all he can do to help you look your best." So in the summer of 2002, I took the big leap and underwent facial surgery that included both a laser peel and a facelift.

Afterward, my recovery was going great. Of course, my face was red and swollen, and I had to keep a greasy ointment on my face at all times to aid in the healing process. Nevertheless, in my mind's eye, I could see a more beautiful me on the other side of my recovery!

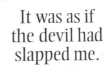

It was as if the devil had slapped me.

Then while recovering from my surgery, I experienced a setback. One day soon after the surgery, bumps began to break out all over my face. After being without blemishes on my face for twenty-five years, suddenly I had a red, swollen, greasy face that was also covered with bumps! It was as if the devil had slapped me. After taking this big step toward trying to do something about those scars, I looked worse than ever.

> The doctors can change your face, but they *cannot* change your soul!

Before I go further, let me back up to explain something that had been happening throughout the previous year be-fore my facial surgery. Jesus had been opening my eyes to what was in my soul. (The doctors can change your face, but they *cannot* change your soul!)

The Lord took me back to a day when I was an eleven-year-old girl living in Oklahoma. I was walking around the house with my head held high and my voice booming through every room. I was singing as if I owned the whole world! I remember it so well.

Over the years, I had watched the way my husband and my sons carry themselves as they walk up to the platform to speak. It's as if they are taking the whole stage as their territory for Jesus! Their freedom had exposed my own bondage. I would think to myself, *If only I could be as free as Rick, Paul, Phillip, and Joel!*

But when the Lord brought back that memory of me as a young girl, singing with such complete abandonment, I realized something: Back then, I'd possessed the same kind of boldness that I saw in Rick and the boys! Through my years of suffering with that horrific skin condition, including all the ridicule I'd endured and my feelings of being less than other people, the enemy had stolen my boldness from me. But now I knew there was a time when I had been truly free, and I wanted this freedom back.

The enemy had stolen my boldness from me.

Then one day, the Lord gave me further revelation about myself. I realize now that He was setting me up for a miracle — leading me toward freedom from a type of bondage that I hadn't even known was hindering me all those years!

Sometimes when Jesus is delivering us from something deep in our souls, He does it line upon line and precept upon precept. His work in me was like this. First, He healed me. Second, when I was twenty-eight years old, He gave me a loving husband who wanted the best for me. Third, He revealed to me what I didn't know about myself — that there had been a time when I was free. Fourth, He continued to give me more revelation from His Word.

Someone had given me some tapes by Derek Prince, and I began listening to them. Brother Prince said that when Jesus died on the Cross, He took our shame and gave us His glory. As I listened, I thought to myself, *There is a lot of difference between shame and glory. I want to experience that glory.*

> Could the reason be that I carried a hidden sense of shame that I hadn't even realized was there?

Suddenly I remembered that I always

covered my face when I prayed. I would often think to myself, *Why do I always do that? Why do I always cover my face?* Could the reason be that I carried a hidden sense of shame that I hadn't even realized was there?

Psalm 119:105 says, *"Thy word is a lamp unto my feet, and a light unto my path."* The light was beginning to shine brighter and brighter in my heart. God was setting the stage for another miracle.

Delivered From Shame!

Now let's go back to several days after the operation when I was looking at all those bumps on my face and the devil was laughing at me because he thought he had won the victory. *But he hadn't!* Before the surgery, I had taken Communion twice a day for two weeks and prayed that God would do exceedingly abundantly above all I could ask or think. Although I looked worse than ever, I *knew* that my faith was not in vain.

In the middle of this spiritual battle, I was invited for dinner to the house of a couple who are dear friends of mine. Now, in the natural, a person does *not* go out in public looking the way I looked! But although I was ashamed of how I looked, I just apologized to my friends for my appearance, put aside my reluctance to step outside my door, and accepted the invitation.

> Although I looked worse than ever, I *knew* that my faith was not in vain.

The gourmet meal was wonderful, as was the fellowship I enjoyed with the hosts. After the dinner, I asked this couple to pray for me. I desperately wanted those bumps to go away so I could get past the ordeal. Besides, I was scheduled to sing for the Joyce Meyer women's conference in two weeks!

When the husband laid hands on me and prayed, I fell to the floor under the power of the Holy Spirit. This had never happened to me before. The anointing was so strong that I couldn't even get up for a solid hour. I had heard of this happening to others, but this was the first time for me.

> During that hour, Jesus completely delivered me from shame.

During that hour, Jesus took me back in my mind to the years before I'd ever had blemishes on my face. Then He let me see myself as if I had never had a skin problem all the way through junior high school, through high school, and through college. I saw myself live through those years with a clear, unblemished face. I saw myself with my head held high and with a confidence that I was just as good as those around me. During that hour, Jesus completely delivered me from shame.

Only Jesus can go down into someone's soul and take out the poisonous root of a problem that the person doesn't even know is there! It was as if He came up to the prison of shame that had held my soul for so long; put His key of love and power in the keyhole; turned the key; opened the door; and said, *"Denise, come out from there — you are free."*

As I lay on that floor, engulfed in the Presence of the Holy Spirit, Jesus told me, "I am restoring you. I am reestablishing you. I am replenishing you." And when I got up from that floor, I was a new person — healed, delivered, and free to walk in a boldness that I hadn't known for more than three decades. Not only that, but from that moment on, the bumps began to disappear. And by the time of the Joyce Meyer conference, my face was clear!

I am happy with the results of my surgery, but what God did on the inside of me was the real surgery. That was the real transformation. His Spirit came over me in such a way that I was changed forever on the inside.

Jesus bore our shame so He could give us His glory; therefore, no one but He can touch and deliver us to this degree. Only He has the authority and power to bring about this kind of change. And it is only the Holy Spirit who can take what Jesus did on the Cross and cause His deliverance to become a manifested reality in our lives!

2

A Perfect Redemption

I am a different person since that evening when Jesus delivered me from shame. Ever since then, I've known that God wants me to share my testimony with others, along with the message that as children of God, we never have to live under the terrible burden of shame.

Redeemed From Shame

Far too many Christians don't realize that Jesus has already redeemed them from every form of shame and emotional pain. Let's look at what Isaiah 53 has to say about this subject.

> **He [Jesus] is despised and rejected of men; a man of sorrows, and acquainted with grief: and we hid as it were our faces from him; he was despised, and we esteemed him not.**
>
> **Isaiah 53:3**

This verse says that Jesus was "despised and rejected of men." If you've ever been despised or rejected, you can rest assured that Jesus was more despised and rejected than you and I ever were. If you've ever felt sorrow, you can know that He was more acquainted with grief than you or I could ever think of being.

Jesus was acquain-ted with so much grief, so much sorrow, and so much rejection that He has the total authority and power to com-pletely deliver us from all of it. He tast-ed to the absolute limit the deepest,

> **Far too many Christians don't realize that Jesus has already redeemed them from every form of shame.**

dar-kest part of the des-truction of shame that could come to the soul of man so we wouldn't have to remain captive to its chains and tyran-ny.

Coming Out
From the Shadow of Shame

I had the right to be delivered from shame because, according to Isaiah 53:4, Jesus bore my shame for me: *"Surely he hath borne our griefs, and carried our sorrows...."* All those times I felt rejected or was made fun of, I didn't know that Jesus had carried the pain of my shame to the Cross for me. I didn't know that He could take that shame out of me and cause me to live in such freedom that it would be as if shame never existed in my life. I also had no idea that by carrying the shame of those experiences, I myself would put a lid on my life that would keep me from fulfilling the highest call God had for me.

> Jesus is a mighty Deliverer.

God sent Jesus to take your shame from you through Jesus' terrible suffering on the Cross. If you have lived under the shadow of shame, you need to know something: *You don't have to live with that shame one more minute!* Jesus is a mighty Deliverer. He can go deep into your heart where no one else can reach to heal you of past hurts and set you free once and for all!

Isaiah 54:4 goes on to say, *"...Yet we did esteem him stricken, smitten of God, and afflicted."*

Do you know what it means to be "smitten of God"? It's as if God put His foot on Jesus and crushed Him as someone might throw a cigarette on the ground and crush it under his heel. The Father punished all wickedness in Jesus so it could no longer have any authority over us. Sin, sickness, and pain lost all their power when Jesus bore them on the Cross and went on to conquer death, hell, and the grave. He conquered shame; He conquered fear; He conquered rejection; He conquered grief — Jesus conquered it *all*!

But he was wounded for our transgressions, he was bruised for our iniquities: the chastisement of our peace was upon him; and with his stripes we are healed.

Isaiah 53:5

> There is One who heals, and His name is Jesus.

Has anyone ever hit or bruised you, either physically or emotionally? Well, you can know that Jesus was bruised more than you could ever imagine. And why did He allow Himself to go through all that suffering? To heal us from all physical and emotional bruises, wounds, and cuts. His suffering was for *us*.

Sometimes life can seem as if we are walking naked through rose bushes; we simply get all cut up. But there is One who heals, and His name is Jesus. No matter how many cuts and bruises this world may have inflicted on us, Jesus can heal them all.

Now notice the last part of verse 5: *"...The chastisement of our peace was upon him; and with his stripes we are healed."* Anything that would ever steal our peace lost its power in Jesus' death and resurrection. He completely punished every damnable thing the devil wants to put on us, and then He rose victorious over it! Therefore, Jesus has the absolute right to deliver us from every single enemy of peace — *including shame!*

Isaiah 53 goes on to say much more about what Jesus went through in order to redeem us from our sins:

All we like sheep have gone

astray; we have turned every one to his own way; and the Lord hath laid on him the iniquity of us all.

He was oppressed, and he was afflicted, yet he opened not his mouth: he is brought as a lamb to the slaughter, and as a sheep before her shearers is dumb, so he openeth not his mouth.

He was taken from prison and from judgment: and who shall declare his generation? for he was cut off out of the land of the living: for the transgression of my people was he stricken.

And he made his grave with the wicked, and with the rich in his death; because he had done no violence, neither was any deceit in his mouth.

Yet it pleased the Lord to bruise him; he hath put him to grief: when thou shalt make his soul an offering for sin, he shall see his seed, he shall prolong his days, and the pleasure of the Lord shall prosper in his hand.

He shall see of the travail of his soul, and shall be satisfied: by his knowledge shall my righteous servant justify many; for he shall bear their iniquities.

Therefore will I divide him a portion with the great, and he shall divide the spoil with the strong; because he hath poured out his soul unto death: and he was numbered with the transgressors; and he bare the sin of many, and made intercession for the transgressors.

Isaiah 53:6-12

Why did it please the Lord to bruise Jesus

and to put Him to grief (v. 10)? Because when the Father looked down the corridors of time and saw you and me, He knew He'd have the right and the power to deliver us from anything the devil put on us, as long as His Son completed the work of redemption He had been sent to fulfill.

Jesus Bore
Our Emotional Wounds

Perhaps you have never really looked hard to see how utterly ridiculed, debased, and crushed Jesus was by the high priest and by the Roman soldiers. I want to focus on some of the horrific things Jesus endured in those dark hours before His death. It is important that you realize what He went through so you could live free from shame.

First, consider this: No one stood with

Jesus in His greatest hour of need. Even the disciples deserted Him when He needed them the most. So if you've ever felt like you were abandoned and left standing alone, Jesus paid for that as well so you can experience joy rather than sorrow and grief. What a powerful salvation you have been given!

> No one stood with Jesus in His greatest hour of need.

Another example can be found in Mark 15:13-15:

And they cried out again, Crucify him.

Then Pilate said unto them, Why, what evil hath he done? And they cried out the more exceedingly, Crucify him.

And so Pilate, willing to content

the people, released Barabbas unto them, and delivered Jesus, when he had scourged him, to be crucified.

Have you ever seen someone else get the good that you deserved?

Has anyone ever wronged you? Have you ever seen someone else get the good that you deserved? Well, think of Jesus! He could have called 10,000 angels to deli-ver Him from the mob that screamed, "Crucify Him! Let the criminal go free, and crucify Him!" But He didn't. Instead, Jesus just kept laying down His rights, His freedom, and His deliverance from all that suffering and continued to trust the Father so you and I could go free.

You may feel like you've been treated

unfairly, but Jesus went so much further, enduring untold punishment for your sin, even though He Himself was without sin. He did that so you could have joy and power and authority and confidence in the unfair situation *you* face.

Jesus already stood in our place and gave us the right to experience victory! Now it's up to you and me to believe it and take that victory into our lives every day.

And the soldiers led him away into the hall, called Praetorium; and they call together the whole band.

And they clothed him with purple, and platted a crown of thorns, and put it about his head,

And began to salute him, Hail, King of the Jews!

Redeemed From Shame

These Roman soldiers were big, muscular men who were used to carrying heavy armor. When they placed that crown of thorns on Jesus, they didn't just place it nicely on top of His hair; they *crammed* that crown into His head as hard as they could. These soldiers were trying to be as obnoxious and mean and cruel as they could be!

To add as much humiliation as possible to their mockery of Jesus, the soldiers also started spitting on Him. I want you to understand this picture. Have you ever seen rude people bring up the phlegm out of their throat and then

> Jesus already stood in our place and gave us the right to experience victory!

42

spit? This was the kind of spitting that these soldiers were inflicting on Jesus. In my husband Rick's book *Sparkling Gems From the Greek*, he describes just how humiliating it was for Jesus to go through this kind of treatment:

> In that culture and time, spitting in one's face was considered to be the strongest thing you could do to show utter disgust, repugnance, dislike, or hatred for someone. When someone spattered his spit on another person's face, that spit was meant to humiliate, demean, debase, and shame that person. To make it worse, the offender would usually spit hard and close to the person's face, making it all the more humiliating.[1]

The Roman soldiers had the freedom to

---

[1] Rick Renner, *Sparkling Gems From the Greek* (Tulsa: Teach All Nations, 2003), p. 236.

spit as much as they wanted on Jesus. The spittle of those filthy, rude Roman soldiers was running down the face of our Lord, but He didn't say a word. If you've ever been embarrassed, humiliated, or made fun of, Jesus has gone much deeper!

The soldiers also kept hitting Jesus as hard as they could, but still He didn't say a word. Then they got on their knees before the One they had spit on and beaten, and they pretended to worship Him. Rick des-cribes the scene, which is also related in Matthew 27:27-29:

> With a discarded royal robe about Jesus' shoulders, a crown of thorns set so deeply into His head that blood drenched His face, and a reed from Pilate's ponds or fountains stuck in His right hand, "...they bowed the

knee before him, and mocked him, saying, Hail, King of the Jews!" The word "bowed" is the Greek word *gonupeteo*, meaning *to fall down upon one's knees*. One by one, the cohort of soldiers passed before Jesus, dramatically and comically dropping to their knees in front of Him as they laughed at and mocked Him.[2]

> You do not have to hide under the shadow of shame.

I'm telling you, friend, freedom and victory are available to you because of all that Jesus suffered on your behalf on that day. You have no right to hide your ministry, your talent, or any other gift God gave you, for He has paid the complete price for any emotional wound you could ever carry! You

2 Ibid., pp. 263-264.

do not have to hide under the shadow of shame.

The Ultimate Price

Mark 15:20 tells us what happened next: *"And when they had mocked him, they took off the purple from him, and put his own clothes on him, and led him out to crucify him."* These soldiers had treated Jesus as if He were nothing — just dirt under their feet. Rick stresses this point:

> When I read of what Jesus endured during the time before He was sent to be crucified, it simply overwhelms me. Jesus committed no sin and no crime, nor was any guile ever found in His mouth; yet He was judged more severely than the worst of criminals. Even hardened criminals would not

have been put through such grueling treatment. And just think — all this happened before He was nailed to that wooden Cross — the lowest, most painful, debasing manner in which a criminal could be executed in the ancient world![3]

Jesus had already endured unspeakable pain and humiliation at the hands of the chief priests and their followers and of the Roman soldiers. Now the soldiers nailed the sinless One to a Cross that stood between two thieves!

And with him they crucify two thieves; the one on his right hand, and the other on his left.

And the scripture was fulfilled, which saith, And he was numbered with the transgressors.

---

3 Ibid., p. 255.

Redeemed From Shame

Mark 15:27,28

How many of us are willing to submit without a word to being wronged when we're right? Jesus did. He wasn't just right; He was absolutely blameless and without sin. Yet He allowed Himself to be identified with *our* sin so we would not be judged as we deserved.

And they that passed by railed on him, wagging their heads, and saying, Ah, thou that destroyest the temple, and buildest it in three days,

Save thyself, and come down from the cross.

Likewise also the chief priests mocking said among themselves with the scribes, He saved others; himself he cannot save.

Redeemed From Shame

Mark 15:29-31

Jesus could have saved Himself totally, but He knew He had to pay the ultimate price for our freedom. So often we want to be treated right and to have people respect us, but Jesus laid down *all* His rights so we could be free.

Jesus paid the complete and ultimate price so we could walk in freedom and victory, even when the enemy uses people or circumstances to cause us shame and hurt. We live in a cursed world filled with imperfect people, and at times evil

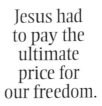

Jesus had to pay the ultimate price for our freedom.

will come out of them against us. But we can be like Jesus in every situation be-cause He

> ## Shame and fear have no right to stay on us!
>
>

gave Him-self to us. He paid the full price.

When Jesus cried out, *"It is finished!"* from the Cross, God marked the debt "Paid in Full." Therefore, every time we're temp-ted to feel sorry for ourselves or to be ashamed or fearful, we need to remember the price Jesus paid for our peace. Shame and fear have no right to stay on us! We can boldly say to ourselves and the devil, "I'm not pay-ing for that, for it's already been paid in full!"

His Triumph Is *Our* Triumph!

Revelation chapter 1 gives us a picture of the risen Jesus who triumphed over death, hell, and the grave.

And in the midst of the seven candlesticks one like unto the Son of man, clothed with a garment down to the foot, and girt about the paps with a golden girdle.

His head and his hairs were white like wool, as white as snow; and his eyes were as a flame of fire;

And his feet like unto fine brass, as if they burned in a furnace; and his voice as the sound of many waters.

And he had in his right hand seven stars: and out of his mouth went a sharp twoedged sword: and his countenance was as the sun shineth in his strength.

And when I saw him, I fell at his feet as dead. And he laid his right hand upon me, saying unto me, Fear not; I am the first and the last:

   I am he that liveth, and was dead;
and, behold, I am alive for evermore,
Amen; and have the keys of hell and
of death.

Revelation 1:13-18

*This is the glorious Savior who has utterly
redeemed us from shame!*

As children of God, we are free to walk
out of the prison of shame and rejection
once and for all, for Jesus' triumph has now
become *our* triumph. We can claim our
rightful inheritance to walk in holy boldness
through this life, for we have been made
wholly righteous through the precious blood
of Jesus.

3

Deliverance Comes
As We Seek the Lord

God touched me in a very deep way that evening in 2002 when I was praying with my friends. It was a night I will never forget, for I was touched by His mighty power. That night reminds me of the words to the famous old song, "He Touched Me":

Redeemed From Shame

"He touched me,
O, He touched me,
And, O, the joy that filled my soul.
Something happened, and now I know.
He touched me and made me whole."[4]

It was as if God took out an awful barrier that had held my mind and emotions in chains and bondage. A very heavy burden I had been carrying since I was twelve years old was removed from me that night forever. Glory to His name!

As Psalm 34:4,5 tells us, God is our Deliverer from *all* our fears and our sense of shame:

I sought the Lord, and he heard me,
and delivered me from all my fears.

They looked unto him, and were
lightened: and their faces were not
ashamed.

[4] William J. Gaither, 1963.

Redeemed From Shame

Look at how both of those verses start out: *"I sought the Lord"* and *"They looked unto him."* So often we want God to do everything instantly. We don't want to wait; we don't want to seek or search. Our flesh wants it *now*!

But most of the time, deliverance in deep character issues comes with time as we keep seeking and looking unto Jesus. Our deliverance does *not* come through analyzing our problems over and over again in our minds for years. Please believe me — I tried that, and it does not work. This kind of worry and incessant analyzing only leaves us more confused. On the contrary, our an-swer is found by seeking the Lord, making time out of our busy schedule to

So often we want God to do everything instantly.

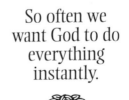

find Him. He alone is our Answer. He alone is our Deliverer.

> Our deliverance does not come through analyzing our problems in our minds.

Now look at the results of seeking the Lord in the last part of both verses. Verse 4 says that God *"...deli-vered me from all my fears,"* and in verse 5, those who looked to the Lord *"...were lightened: and their faces were not ashamed."* Do you see that we can't stay the same if we are seeking and looking for God?

Just for a moment, imagine yourself looking at Jesus. As you look at Him, at first glance you may want to look away because He is so holy and because His light reveals every area of darkness in your life.

But as you keep looking, you see that there is no condemnation in Jesus' eyes; rather, love and mercy are flowing from His Presence. You only sense Him wanting you to draw near. Now you don't *want* to look away. In fact, you *can't* look away, for you are captivated by His compassion for you. You sense so much comfort and peace flowing from Him in your direction.

> There is no condemnation in Jesus' eyes.

As you experience Jesus' loving touch, your heart can see that you are totally accepted by Him, and all you want to do is continue to bask in His Presence. Before you know it, you can't even think about yourself or your problem. Your heart is open, your spirit soaring like an eagle. You see yourself as *He* sees you — completely accepted in the Beloved. There is now no room for fear or shame, for you have been conquered by His loving Presence. When you walk away, you have been changed forever.

Oh, how God wants us to experience His great love for us just like that every moment of our lives! Because of His suffering on the Cross and in hell, He paid the ultimate price for us to experience His loving presence. This is possible not by any work of righteousness that *we* have done, but by trusting in what *He* has done.

So don't listen to the lies of the devil about your past. Don't let him convince you to give up. Instead, seek God's face, and listen to the loving words of truth from God's Spirit that are there for you. Jesus' flesh was not ripped apart in vain. It was for your deliverance and freedom to become the person God planned for you to be!

Redeemed From Shame

Jesus took all your shame and fear so you wouldn't have to be tormented by its wicked hold. In exchange, He freely offered you His glory and healing power. All you have to do is receive by faith what He has already given you. You are free from the bondage of shame in Him. *Now it's time to LIVE free in Jesus' name!*

Prayer for Freedom
From Shame

Maybe you have beautiful skin and have never suffered from cystic acne. But perhaps you were made fun of or rejected in the past for some other reason. Maybe you were even sexually or physically abused, and you can sense that your life has been affected by the horrible shadow of shame. If so, I urge you to pray this prayer from your heart as your first step toward your freedom.

Dear Heavenly Father, I come to You in Jesus' name. Thank You for the terrible suffering that Jesus experienced for me. I see that He took all my shame and wants to give me glory. Thank You, my Savior, for becoming my shame in Your suffering. I believe You did it for me because You love me so much.

I humble myself before You now to believe Your Word and to have faith that I can be free through the blood of Jesus. His sacrifice is enough for me, and I don't have to hide anymore. Jesus, You have set me free to hold my head high and become the person You made me to be.

Father, I receive my freedom through Jesus' blood. His blood is enough for me. I am Your child, Father, and I know this is Your will for me. Thank You, Father. I love You. I know You hear me. I pray this in the precious name of Jesus. Amen.

For Further Information

For all book orders, please contact:

Teach All Nations
*A book company anointed to take God's Word
to you and to the nations of the world.*

A Division of
Rick Renner Ministries
P. O. Box 702040
Tulsa, OK 74170-2040
Phone: 877-281-8644
Fax: 918-496-3278

*For prayer requests
or for further information about this ministry,
please write or call
the Rick Renner Ministries office
nearest you (see following page).*

All USA Correspondence:
Rick Renner Ministries
P. O. Box 702040
Tulsa, OK 74170-2040
(918) 496-3213
Or 1-800-RICK-593
E-mail: renner@renner.org
Website: www.renner.org

Riga Office:
Rick Renner Ministries
Unijas 99
Riga LV-1084
Latvia
(371) 780-2150

Moscow Office:
Rick Renner Ministries
P. O. Box 14
Moscow 109316
Russia
7 (095) 727-1470

Kiev Office:
Rick Renner Ministries
P. O. Box 205
Kiev 01025
Ukraine
380 (44) 248-7254

Oxford Office:
Rick Renner Ministries
Box 7, 266 Banbury Road
Oxford OX2 7DL
England
44 (1865) 355509
E-mail: europe@renner.org

NOTE:

*To order a complete audio, video,
and book catalog,
please contact our offices in
Tulsa or Oxford.*

About the Author

Denise Renner was raised in Miami, Okla-homa. Born into a Southern Baptist family, Denise gave her heart to Jesus Christ at the age of seven. Although young when her decision was made to follow Jesus, Denise understood what she was doing and began her lifetime commitment of serving the Lord Jesus Christ.

While attending a local college in Miami, Oklahoma, Denise was doing her best to serve the Lord with all her heart, yet feeling powerless to witness. Sitting on a street curb outside her college classroom in 1972, Denise opened her heart to the Lord and was gloriously filled with the Holy Spirit. The young Baptist girl was now connected to the power of God. In that moment, her life was changed forever as God set her life on a totally different course.

Immediately after being filled with the Spirit, Denise's heart was set on fire to win souls for

Jesus Christ. Testifying to unbelievers became the driving desire of her heart and soul. For twelve years, she studied and performed opera at various colleges and opera companies, but the surpassing passion of her heart was to marry a man of God and serve with him in the work of the ministry.

This dream was realized when Denise married Rick Renner in 1981. Rick and Denise ministered widely throughout the United States for several years before answering God's call in 1991 to move their family to the former Soviet Union and plunge into the heart of its newly emerging Church. Today Denise works alongside her husband Rick to see the Gospel preached, leadership trained, and the Church established throughout the world.

Rick Renner Ministries has offices in England, Latvia, Russia, Ukraine, and the United States. Rick, Denise, and their three sons live in Moscow, Russia.